2 GRRRLS™

I Love My Life

2 GRRRLS™ Words to Live By

compiled by the Grrrls of 2 GRRRLS

SCHOLASTIC INC.

New York   Toronto   London   Auckland   Sydney
Mexico City   New Delhi   Hong Kong

ISBN 0-439-18738-9
Copyright © 2001 by 2 GRRRLS, Inc.
Cover and interior design by Louise Bova

Published by Scholastic Inc. All rights reserved.

SCHOLASTIC and associated logos are trademarks and/or registered trademarks of Scholastic Inc. 2 GRRRLS and logo faces and all related characters and elements are trademarks and/or registered trademarks of 2 GRRRLS, Inc.
BE THE GIRL YOU WANNA BE
is a trademark of 2 GRRRLS, Inc.

12 11 10 9 8 7 6 5 4 3 2 1   1 2 3 4 5 6/0

Printed in the U.S.A.
First Scholastic printing, March 2001

Table of Contents

Hi, Hello, How Are Ya?

If you are a girl who wants to make the most out of her life, then this is the book for you. You might be trying to figure out what's most important to you. Or you might want to discover what really makes you the person you are. Maybe you feel like you've got most of those things pretty much figured out. No matter what is on your mind, this is a book that will make you think. It will inspire you to live the life that's right for you. When it comes to making your dreams come true, you can't just go with the flow. You've got to think about who you are, what you want to do, and make it happen.

Not only does this book include amazing quotes, it also gives you the chance to write down your own words of wisdom. Take the blank pages to put your pen to paper and record what you think. Write on, girl!

Be the girl you wanna be, and fill the world with inspiration!

Creativity

Creativity is a way of expressing

your personality and showing other

people the way you see things.

It's not only painting a picture,

but it's also writing a letter

or the way you wear your clothes.

Creativity is an outward

expression of who you are

on the inside.

Imagination is the highest kite you can fly.

Lauren Bacall, actor

Any activity becomes creative when the doer cares about doing it right, or doing it better.

John Updike, author

Creativity is allowing oneself to make mistakes. Art is knowing which ones to keep.

Scott Adams, cartoonist

Discovery consists in seeing what everyone else has seen and thinking what no one else has thought.

Albert Szent-Gyorgi von Nagyrapolt, Nobel Prize winner in Physiology and Medicine (1937)

Creativity comes from trust. Trust your instincts. And never hope more than you work.

Rita Mae Brown, author

A hunch is creativity trying to tell you something.

Frank Capra, film director

Imagination is more important than knowledge.

Albert Einstein, physicist

When I can no longer create anything, I'll be done for.

Coco Chanel, fashion designer

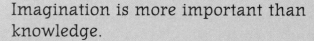

The voyage of discovery is not in seeking new land-scapes but in having new eyes.

Marcel Proust, author

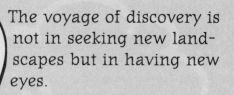

8

Wisdom

Wisdom isn't just knowing the

answers to questions you are asked

in class. It's being able to use your

heart and your head together

to figure out what really makes

sense. Wisdom is something

you earn by keeping your

eyes, ears, and heart open to

life's experiences.

Wisdom begins in wonder.

Socrates, philosopher

The doors of wisdom are never shut.

Benjamin Franklin, statesperson,
philosopher, and inventor

I am never afraid of what I know.

Anna Sewell, author

It is characteristic of wisdom not to
do desperate things.

Henry David Thoreau,
author

The fool doth think he is wise, but the wise man knows himself to be a fool.

William Shakespeare, playwright and poet

The important thing is not to stop questioning.

Albert Einstein, physicist

When you don't have knowledge and understanding, then fear rises in you. Knowledge . . . gives people the tools to deal with change.

Madonna, singer and actor

Nothing in life is to be feared. It is only to be understood.

Marie Curie, chemist

It is the mark of an educated mind to be able to entertain a thought without accepting it.

Aristotle, philosopher

Wisdom is not knowing the right answer,
but seeing all the possibilities.

One of the Grrrls

Intelligent people think for
themselves and make their own
decisions, but truly brilliant people listen to
and learn from the advice of others.

One of the Grrrls

Our feelings are our most genuine path to
knowledge.

Audré Lorde, poet

The wisest person is not the one who is quickest to see through a thing; rather it is the person who will see a thing through.

One of the Grrrls

A wise person never knows all; only fools know everything.

African proverb

Knowledge can be communicated but not wisdom.

Hermann Hesse, author

Life is a persistent teacher. It will keep repeating lessons until we learn.

One of the Grrrls

Individuality

Individuality is ultra-important. Individuality is a willingness to be yourself and to stand up for what you believe in — no matter what other people think.

Don't be afraid to be yourself. Be afraid not to.

One of the Grrrls

Always be a first-rate version of yourself, instead of a second-rate version of somebody else.

Judy Garland, singer and actor

I like being unconventional.

Florence Griffith Joyner, athlete

Say what you think.

One of the Grrrls

Be true to yourself.
One of the Grrrls

Every person is a gem — you just have to find the shiny parts.
One of the Grrrls

Independence is happiness.
Susan B. Anthony, suffragist

Stand for something — or you'll fall for anything.
Unknown

Cherish forever what makes you unique,
'cuz you're really a yawn if it goes.

Bette Midler, singer and actor

What a lovely surprise to discover how
unlonely being alone can be.

Ellen Burstyn, actor

Who You Are

Knowing who you are

means keeping in touch with

what makes you you.

That's your identity. Hang on

tight — it's the most impor-

tant thing you've got.

It belongs to you and

no one else.

25

Character consists of what you do on the third and fourth tries.

James A. Michener, author

I've been trying to find the word that says what I need to be in life. "Brave" is the only word. It's the only thing that I ask myself to be.

Sandra Bullock, actor

Character cannot be developed in ease and quiet. Only through experiences of trial and suffering can the soul be strength-ened, vision cleared, ambition inspired, and success achieved.

Helen Keller, lecturer and essayist

It's easier to say what we believe than to be what we believe.

One of the Grrrls

What you see in the mirror is only part of the picture.

One of the Grrrls

Know your talents, and recognize the talents of others.

One of the Grrrls

Know yourself.

Socrates, philosopher

What lies behind us and what lies before us are tiny matters compared to what lies within us.

Ralph Waldo Emerson, author and philosopher

Great souls have wills; feeble ones have only wishes.

Chinese proverb

It all starts with self-reflection. Then you can know and empathize more profoundly with someone else.

Shirley MacLaine, actor and author

We relish news of our heroes, forgetting that we are extraordinary to somebody, too.

Helen Hayes, actor

Be careless in your dress if you must, but keep a tidy soul.

Mark Twain, author and humorist

Friendship

During the best and worst of times you want your friends by your side. They're the ones who will share your joy and pain. Friendship is a commitment of the soul, a promise of the heart. True friendship is fortifying — one of life's greatest gifts.

A friend is someone who reaches for your hand and touches your heart.

One of the Grrrls

If you want to be listened to, you should put in time listening.

Marge Piercy, author

Friends are the family we choose for ourselves.

Edna Buchanan, author

I get by with a little help from my friends.

The Beatles, musicians

There is no color to the hand of friendship.

One of the Grrrls

Friendship doubles our joy and divides our grief.

Swedish proverb

It's easier to lose a fight than to lose a friend.

One of the Grrrls

Constant use will not wear ragged the fabric of friendship.

Dorothy Parker, author and critic

Friends are like stars in the night sky — the more you have, the brighter your life will be.

One of the Grrrls

The most called-upon requisite of a friend is an accessible ear.

Maya Angelou, author and poet

You cannot be friends upon any other terms than upon the terms of equality.

Woodrow Wilson, twenty-eighth president of the United States

The only way to have a friend is to be one.

Ralph Waldo Emerson, author and philosopher

True friendship is an understanding. It's when two people believe in each other and support each other's dreams.

One of the Grrrls

Friendship is like a flower that blossoms through all weather and never wilts or fades.

One of the Grrrls

If we would build on a sure foundation in friendship we must love friends for their sake rather than our own.

Charlotte Brontë, author

If I don't have friends, then I ain't got nothing.

Billie Holiday, singer

Don't wait for others to be friendly, show them how.

One of the Grrrls

A friend gathers all the pieces and gives them back in the right order.

Toni Morrison, author

As long as we sweeten another's pain, our lives are not in vain.

Helen Keller, lecturer and essayist

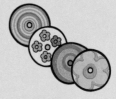

Talk is a refuge.

Zora Neale Hurston, author

Love

Some people say love

is when you have the

same deep hope for others that

you have for yourself.

Giving love is just as

good as receiving it,

and the rewards are endless.

Love is really

an awesome thing.

Love has nothing to do with what you are expecting to get, only with what you are expected to give . . . which is everything.

Katharine Hepburn, actor

To love is not to look at each other, but to look together in the same direction.

Antoine de Saint-Exupéry, author and aviator

Love and magic have a great deal in common. They enrich the soul, delight the heart. And they both take practice.

Nora Roberts, author

What we have once enjoyed we can never lose. All that we love deeply becomes a part of us.

Helen Keller, lecturer and essayist

Who so loves
Believes the impossible.

Elizabeth Barrett Browning, poet

The more I wonder . . . the more I love.

Alice Walker, author

The Eskimos have fifty-two names for snow
because it is important to them; there ought
to be as many for love.

Margaret Atwood, author

Love liberates everything.

Maya Angelou, author and poet

When you love someone all your saved-up
wishes start coming out.

Elizabeth Bowen, author

Love dies only when growth stops.

Pearl S. Buck, author

When people care for you and cry for you, they can straighten out your soul.

Langston Hughes, author and poet

To love means you also trust.

Joan Baez, singer

Love lights more fires than hate can extinguish.

Ella Wheeler-Wilcox, poet and journalist

I have learned not to worry about love, but to honor its coming with all my heart.

Alice Walker, author

I still miss those I loved who are no longer with me but I find I am grateful for having loved them. The gratitude has finally conquered the loss.

Rita Mae Brown, author

Where there is great love there are always miracles.

Willa Cather, author

Why is the measure of love loss?

Jeanette Winterson, author

If grass can grow through cement, love can find you anywhere.

Cher, singer

A real princess believes in love and fairy tales.

Rella, one of the Grrrls

Community

Your community is all the people around you. It is your family and your closest group of friends. But it is also your soccer team and the rival team. A community includes everyone in your school and neighborhood, and each community is filled with many kinds of people, and the world is filled with many communities. How you see your community says a lot about you. Although we have personal goals for success and happiness, we must keep in mind our role in our community and in the world.

One person can make a difference and every person should try.

John F. Kennedy, thirty-fifth president of the United States

The strength of a nation derives from the integrity of the home.

Confucius, philosopher

You leave home to seek your fortune and, when you get it, you go home and share it with your family.

Anita Baker, singer

As long as you keep a person down, some part of you has to be down there to hold the person down, so it means you cannot soar as you otherwise might.

Marian Anderson, singer

Your family is a patchwork quilt — no matter how different each person is, your lives are all sewn together. Each square is beautiful, but the more squares in the quilt, the warmer it will be.

One of the Grrrls

Never doubt that a small group of thought-ful, committed citizens can change the world. Indeed, it is the only thing that ever has.

Margaret Mead, anthropologist

Humankind has not woven the web of life. We are but one thread within it. Whatever we do to the web, we do to ourselves. All things are bound together. All things connect.

Chief Seattle, Suquamish chief

It's real nice being important, but it's more important to be nice.

One of the Grrrls

Your family is your past, your present, and your future.

One of the Grrrls

Forgive your enemies. Nothing annoys them so much!

Unknown

To the world you may be one person, but to one person you may be the world.

Taylor Hanson, musician

Snowflakes, leaves, humans, plants, raindrops, stars, molecules, microscopic entities all come in communities. The singular cannot in reality exist.

Paula Gunn Allen, author

Dreams

Dreams don't only play across your eyelids while you are asleep. True dreams are the ones you have written for yourself and hold deep in your heart — the ideas you have of who you want to be and what you want to do in the future. If you believe in your dreams, you can make them reality.

Wild ones . . . follow their dreams until they come true.

Looie, one of the Grrrls

Go confidently in the direction of your dreams. Live the life you've always imagined.

Henry David Thoreau, author

Hold fast to dreams for if dreams die, life is a broken-winged bird that cannot fly.

Langston Hughes, author and poet

Far away there in the sunshine are my highest aspirations. I may not reach them, but I can look up and see their beauty, believe in them, and try to follow where they lead.

Louisa May Alcott, author

So many of our dreams at first seem impossible, then they seem improbable, and then, when we summon the will, they soon become inevitable.

Christopher Reeve, actor and medical research activist

Without leaps of imagination, or dreaming, we lose the excitement of possibilities. Dreaming, after all, is a form of planning.

Gloria Steinem, author and feminist activist

It takes a lot of courage to show your dreams to someone else.

Erma Bombeck, author and humorist

What really breaks a heart is taking away its dreams.

Pearl S. Buck, author

Hitch your wagon to a star.

Ralph Waldo Emerson, author and philosopher

If you give your dreams wings,
they will carry you to new
heights.

One of the Grrrls

We are the music makers, and we
are the dreamers of dreams.

*Willy Wonka, from <u>Willy Wonka and the
Chocolate Factory</u> by Roald Dahl*

If you can dream it you can do it.

*Walt Disney, animator and studio
executive*

Self-Worth

You can't put a price

on yourself, but you

can see value in who

you are. Self-worth is

all about having

pride and believing

in yourself.

It is the Key

to success.

59

Beauty comes from within.

Tutti, one of the Grrrls

Remember, no one can make you feel inferior without your consent.

Eleanor Roosevelt, humanitarian, diplomat, and former first lady

Don't compromise yourself. You are all you've got.

Janis Joplin, singer

It took me a long time not to judge myself through someone else's eyes.

Sally Field, actor

It is not what lies behind us or what lies before us but what lies within us.

One of the Grrrls

If someone tells you that you cannot do something and you believe it, they are right.

Carol Burnett, actor and comedian

Keep away from people who try to belittle your ambitions. Small people always do that, but the really great make you feel that you, too, can become great.

Mark Twain, author and humorist

If you don't believe in your-self, you never get anywhere.

Mariah Carey, singer

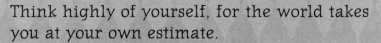

Think highly of yourself, for the world takes you at your own estimate.

One of the Grrrls

Friendship with oneself is all important, because without it, one cannot be friends with anyone else in the world.

Eleanor Roosevelt, humanitarian, diplomat, and former first lady

Love yourself first and everything else falls into line. You really have to love yourself to get anything done in this world.

Lucille Ball, actor and comedian

There is nothing noble about being superior to some other person. The true nobility is in being superior to your previous self.

Hindu proverb

It is easy to live for others; everybody does. I call on you to live for yourselves.

Ralph Waldo Emerson, author and philosopher

I began to understand that self-esteem isn't everything; it's just that there's nothing without it.

Gloria Steinem, author and feminist activist

Other people may not have high expectations of me, but I have high expectations for myself.

Shannon Miller, athlete

Making Decisions

Making decisions can be hard. It's not always easy knowing what the right decision is, and sometimes there is no right answer. But decisions can change things, for better or for worse. You have to think things through and do what is best for you. In the end, you need to know you tried to make the right decision and learn from your mistake if you were wrong.

In any moment of decision the best thing you can do is the right thing, the next best thing is the wrong thing, and the worst thing you can do is nothing.

Theodore Roosevelt, twenty-sixth president of the United States

I have to make my own decisions and live by them.

Mariah Carey, singer

If you listen to your conscience it will serve you as no other friend you'll know.

Loretta Young, actor

Do the right thing.

Spike Lee, actor and film director

It's not what's right or wrong but what's right for me.

Drew Barrymore, actor

If you seek what is honorable . . . all the other things you could not imagine come as a matter of course.

Oprah Winfrey, talk show host and actor

My grand-daddy always used to say: You gotta put somethin' down to pick something up.

C.B. White, soul traveler

Going through my twenties made clear to me that nothing is really as important as the value of your relationships. You can't make a decision based on money. You can't make a decision based on how much fun you think you're going to have. It's strictly about the value of the relationships you build. Then all of that other stuff is going to come naturally.

Will Smith, actor and musician

If you don't make a decision,
time will make it for you.

Unknown

Whatever I do, I want to say that I've done
my best going down whatever path I take.

Joshua Jackson, actor

If you don't like something, change it. If
you can't change it, change your attitude.
Don't complain.

Maya Angelou, author and poet

Trust your instincts.

One of the Grrrls

Be the master of your will and
the slave of your conscience.

Unknown

Outlook on Life

Your life has no definition. It's up to you to define it. You are the author. What will the story of your life be? In order to work toward a happy ending, you need to have a positive outlook. You need to see the world and believe that you have contributions to make. You need to know what you believe. You need to stay true to your beliefs.

I would rather be able to appreciate things I cannot have than to have things I am not able to appreciate.

Elbert Hubbard, author and editor

Honesty is the best policy. You might need to be careful about the best way to tell the truth, but you should never disguise it.

One of the Grrrls

A woman can do anything.

Barbara Walters, journalist

The past is history. The future, a mystery. The present is a gift.

Unknown

Anyone who has never made a mis-take has never tried anything new.

Albert Einstein, physicist

The best and most beautiful things in the world cannot be seen or even touched — they must be felt with the heart.

Helen Keller, lecturer and essayist

They who contemplate the beauty of the earth find reserves of strength that endure as long as life lasts.

Rachel Carson, writer and environmental activist

That it will never come again is what makes life sweet.

Emily Dickinson, poet

You don't get to choose how you're going to die. Or when. You can decide how you're going to live now.

Joan Baez, singer

The time you enjoy wasting is not wasted time.

Bertrand Russell, philosopher

You never know when you are making a memory.

Rickie Lee Jones, singer

My motto is that I enjoy life. I think there's a kind of simplicity to that way of thinking.

Jenna Elfman, actor

I will permit no man to narrow and degrade my soul by making me hate him.

Booker T. Washington, author, educator, and civil rights activist

The rainbows of life follow the storms.

One of the Grrrls

Life is a journey, not a destination. It is only with the Heart that one can see rightly. What is essential is invisible to the eye.

Antoine de Saint-Exupéry, author and aviator

The only limit to our realization of tomorrow will be our doubts of today.

Franklin D. Roosevelt, thirty-second president of the United States

There is more to life than simply increasing its speed.

Mohandas Gandhi, Indian political leader and civil rights advocate

The pessimist sees difficulty in every opportunity. The optimist sees opportunity in every difficulty.

Winston Churchill, former prime minister of Great Britain

People can't change the truth. . . . But the truth can change people.

Unknown

Small steps . . . They don't have to be big steps. They just have to head in the right direction.

Tom Clancy, author

Sometimes you can see a lot by just looking.

Yogi Berra, athlete

Forgiveness is a gift of high value, yet it costs nothing.

Unknown

A smile adds a lot to your face value.

Unknown

There is a vast difference between having to say something and having something to say.

One of the Grrrls

The best preparation for tomorrow is the right use of today.

Unknown

In spite of everything I still believe that people are really good at heart.

Anne Frank, diarist

I don't know what my future holds, but I know who holds my future — me!

One of the Grrrls

When a man points a finger at someone else, he should remember that three of his fingers are pointing at himself.

Unknown

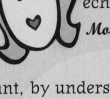

Kind words can be short and easy to speak, but their echoes are truly endless.

Mother Teresa, humanitarian

I want, by understanding myself, to understand others. I want to be all I am capable of becoming.

Katherine Mansfield, author

To think and to be fully alive are the same.

Hannah Arendt, political scientist

Whatever you're ready for is ready for you.

One of the Grrrls

78

Experience and Adventure

WARNING: Experience and adventure can create long-lasting memories and can change your life forever — for the better! The world is a huge place, and there is a lot to learn. Getting hands-on experience is the best way to find out what life is about.

Life moves pretty fast. If you don't stop and take a look around once in a while . . . you could miss it.

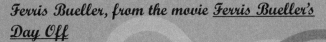

Ferris Bueller, from the movie Ferris Bueller's Day Off

If your experiences would benefit anybody, give them to somebody.

Florence Nightingale, humanitarian

When I look back on it now, I am so glad that the one thing that I had in my life was my belief that everything in life is a learning experience, whether it be positive or negative. If you can see it as a learning experience, you can turn any negative into a positive.

Neve Campbell, actor

Do not be too timid and squeamish about your actions. All life is an experience.

Ralph Waldo Emerson, author and philosopher

I am not afraid of storms for I am learning
how to sail my ship.

Louisa May Alcott, author

Life is either a daring adventure or nothing.

Helen Keller, lecturer and essayist

You cannot create experience. You must
undergo it.

Albert Camus, author and philosopher

Only the wearer knows where the
shoe pinches.

English proverb

Adventure is worthwhile in itself.

Amelia Earhart, aviator

No matter how old you are, you are always
growing — not necessarily in your height,
but in your mind. The more you know and
experience, the more you understand about
the world and how you can contribute.

One of the Grrrls

We turn not older with years, but newer every day.

Emily Dickinson, poet

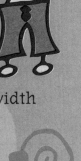

A journey of a thousand miles begins with a single step.

Unknown

I don't want to get to the end of my life and find that I've just lived the length of it. I want to have lived the width of it as well.

Diane Ackerman, author

Experience teaches only the teachable.

Aldous Huxley, author

Life is a book, and you are the author.

One of the Grrrls

My favorite thing to do is to go where I've never been.

Diane Arbus, photographer

Success

There are different kinds of success, and there are different ways to judge success. Success is achieving goals, doing your best, and feeling good about yourself. Just keep in mind that you are the only one who can truly measure your own success.

I have failed over and over again — that is
why I succeed.

Michael Jordan, athlete

All I can do is the best I can.

Drew Barrymore, actor

Some people dream of success, while others
wake up and work hard at it.

One of the Grrrls

The only place SUCCESS comes
before WORK is in the dictionary.

Vidal Sassoon, hairdresser and entrepreneur

Tell me, I will forget. Show me, I may
remember. Involve me, and I will understand.

Chinese proverb

You go, girl. . . . You can be anything you want to be.

Roxy, one of the 2 Grrrls girls

If you have made mistakes . . . there is always another chance for you . . . you may have a fresh start any moment you choose, for this thing we call failure is not the falling down, but the staying down.

Mary Pickford, actor

You may have to fight a battle more than once to win it.

Margaret Thatcher, former prime minister of Great Britain

Obstacles don't have to stop you. If you run into a wall, don't turn around and give up. Figure out how to climb it, go through it, or work around it.

Michael Jordan, athlete

If you don't learn from your mistakes, there's no point in making them.

One of the Grrrls

Always remember that your own resolution to succeed is more important than anything else.

Abraham Lincoln, sixteenth president of the United States

Self-awareness is probably the most important thing in becoming a champion.

Billie Jean King, athlete

Success is not always "getting." It is more often "giving."

Claudia "Lady Bird" Johnson, former first lady

You always pass failure on the way to success.

Mickey Rooney, actor

Success means we go to sleep at night knowing that our talents and abilities were used in a way that served others.

Marianne Williamson, author and spiritual leader

Genius is one percent inspiration and ninety-nine percent perspiration.

Thomas Alva Edison, inventor

If we all did the things we are capable of doing, we would literally astound ourselves.

Thomas Alva Edison, inventor

You've got to do your own growing, no matter how tall your grandfather was.

Irish proverb

I just have to continue to believe in myself.

Vanessa Atler, athlete

Alone we can do so little; together we can do so much.

Helen Keller, lecturer and essayist

Your success is something only you can judge – do not use the scales of others.

One of the Grrrls

Those who dare to fail miserably can achieve greatly.

Robert F. Kennedy, politician

It had long since come to my attention that people of accomplishment rarely sat back and let things happen to them. They went out and happened to things.

Elinor Smith, author and aviator

The reward of a thing well done is to have done it.

Ralph Waldo Emerson, author and philosopher

Work hard, be yourself, and have fun.

Michelle Kwan, athlete

In life, there are no winners or losers . . . just different ways of playing the game.

One of the Grrrls

Failure is impossible.

Susan B. Anthony, suffragist